Funny Business

Funny Business

dictated (but not read)

by

Suds Lonigan

BARNES
& NOBLE
BOOKS
NEW YORK

Some of the cartoons in this book have appeared in the following publications and are reprinted by permission of the artists:

Cartoons on pp. 16, 87, 100 are copyrighted by *The New Yorker.*

This edition published by Barnes & Noble, Inc.
by arrangement with James Charlton Associates.

1993 Barnes & Noble Books

Interior design and typography by Noble Desktop Publishers

ISBN 1-56619-044-4

Printed and bound in the United States of America

M 9 8 7 6 5 4 3 2 1

This is dedicated to a boss I once had who told me that the only way I could get ahead in the company was to get so efficient in my job that she'd look good and get promoted and then I'd be named to replace her. So I did.

•••••••••••

The head of sales was leaving and being replaced by Malcolm, a younger manager. As the retiring executive met Malcolm for the last time, he handed him three sealed envelopes.

"I'm going to do for you what my predecessor did for me, Malcolm. Here are three numbered envelopes. When you run into your first crisis, open the first envelope. When you hit the second major problem, open the next. Save the last envelope for the third crisis. And good luck."

Then he left.

When the first half-year dividend was declared, it was just a fraction of the previous year's earnings. The CEO was furious and demanded an immediate report from every department head. Malcolm realized it was time for action. He opened his desk drawer and ripped open the envelope.

BLAME YOUR PREDECESSOR

When he met with the CEO the next day, he

followed the letter's advice and tore into the man he had replaced. The CEO was satisfied.

Six months later, the year-end sales figures were posted. The numbers were just half the previous years. Again, the CEO was furious and demanded an explanation. Malcolm hurried back to his office and, with trembling hands, opened envelope number two.

REORGANIZE

Following the advice, he presented a new departmental structure and organizational chart to the CEO. New people were to be hired and a dozen were to be replaced. The CEO was happy.

Another six months went by and the new people were producing even less than the old employees. Sales were still down and morale was terrible. The CEO called and in a gruff voice barked, "Get your ass down here, Malcolm." It was time for the last envelope, which he hurriedly opened and read.

PREPARE THREE ENVELOPES...

•••••••••••

There are three things that every man can do better than anyone else. One is coach a football team. The second is judge a beauty contest. The third is write advertising.

Bert Sugar

•••••••••••

The boss walked up behind the bookkeeper who had his feet up on the desk and was reading the newspaper.

"Why aren't you working?" demanded the boss.

"Because I didn't hear you coming!"

•••••••••••

Brenda, the curvaceous blond secretary, was reaching for a pencil she dropped when the boss walked by.

"I appreciate a pat on the back, Mr. Callison," she yelled after him. "But not so low."

•••••••••••

Boss: One who's late when you're early and early when you're late.

•••••••••••

Paula, a young, good-looking, blond secretary, who was rumored to be having an affair, walked past the office coffee cart.

"Look at the Donna Karan dress she's wearing," observed another secretary. "Everyone wonders how she can do it on her boss's salary."

•••••••••••

The owner of the electronics store was showing the new salesman around. "These VCRs we buy for $30 and we sell for $29.95."

"$29.95!" exclaimed the new man. "How do you make any money?"

"That comes when we repair them."

• • • • • • • • • • • •

Two stockbrokers were backpacking in the woods of Maine when a huge black bear suddenly appeared behind them and started ambling along the path. The two quickened their walk, but the bear increased his speed as well. Soon they were sprinting, but the bear kept pace. Suddenly, one of them stopped and opened his backpack.

"What the hell are you doing?" exclaimed the other as he watched his friend change into his running shoes. "If we don't hurry we'll be attacked by that bear."

"I've got a new agenda, Barney. I just realized that I don't have to outrun the bear—I just have to outrun you!"

• • • • • • • • • • • •

"Did you hear Jamie made a killing in the stock market?"

"No, really?"

"Yeah, he shot his broker!"

••••••••••••

The boss stood at the door, tapping his foot as Brokaw walked in.

"Brokaw, you should have been here at nine o'clock!"

"Why, what happened?"

••••••••••••

The salesman looked out the window of the hotel bar at the blinding snow storm raging outside.

"Say bartender, think the roads'll be clear enough in the morning to travel?"

The bartender shrugged. "Depends if you're on salary or commission."

••••••••••••

An advertising agency: 85% confusion, 15% commission.

Fred Allen

• • • • • • • • • • •

"There are two rules to remember around here, Phillips. The first is 'the boss is always right.'"

"What's the second, Mr. Crouse?"

"When the boss is wrong, refer to rule 1!"

• • • • • • • • • • •

"I don't know what your problem is, Ben," Russell said to his brother. "There are a thousand different ways to make money, but there is only one honest way to make money."

"And just what is that, wise guy?"

"Hmmm, I didn't think you'd know."

• • • • • • • • • • •

Overtime: Time spent doing the work in the evening you never quite got round to doing during the day.

John Kelly

• • • • • • • • • • • •

Filing cabinet: A useful container where things can be lost alphabetically.

• • • • • • • • • • • •

"Mr. Atkinson, it was good of you to come and visit me in the hospital," said Smedley. "I'll be out of here just as soon as I can."

"Don't worry about a thing, Smedley. Everyone in the office has promised to pitch in and do your work until you're back. Just as soon as we can figure out what you do!"

• • • • • • • • • • • •

"So Martha, what kind of guy is your new boss?" asked a colleague on the elevator.

Martha rolled her eyes. "You know what boss is spelled backwards?"

"Double S.O.B.!"

•••••••••••

"I'm answering your ad about a job."

"Sit right down young lady," said the personnel director. "As you know, we're looking for someone bright, hard-working, and above all, responsible."

"Oh, that's me, sir. In my last job, whenever something went wrong, they always said I was responsible!"

•••••••••••

"Mr. Haber, I was passed over for the job as the new assistant manager," said John. "Didn't you consider my qualifications?"

Haber put his arm around John's shoulder. "I don't want to talk about your qualifications, my boy. What's past is past."

•••••••••••

I don't want any yes-men around me. I want everyone to tell the truth—even though it costs him his job.

Sam Goldwyn

• • • • • • • • • • • •

Harry was drinking coffee and reading the paper at the coffee shop when his friend Bill walked in.

"Harry, how come you're not at work?"

"Oh, I had a fight with my boss and I won't go back there till he takes back what he said to me."

"And what's that?" asked Bill.

"You're fired!"

"I hope, Reinhardt, that you're not one of those people whose sense of self-worth is defined by their job."

• • • • • • • • • • •

"Hey, Vickie," said Debbie. "Aren't you ever going to take a vacation?"

Vickie shook her head. "I can't get away."

"Why is that? Think the company can't get along without you?"

"They certainly can. That's why I'm not going to take a vacation and let them find out."

• • • • • • • • • • •

Mr. Reasnor, the floor manager, walked up to the counter where two clerks were chatting.

"Harris, Gonzales, can't you find some work to do?"

"Gee, Mr. Reasnor, we're supposed to do the work—and find it too!?"

• • • • • • • • • • •

Money can't buy you friends, but it can buy you a better class of enemy.

Spike Milligan

••••••••••••

"Ben, this is Tim. If you're still out of work, our company is looking for a bookkeeper."

"I am," replied Ben. "But I thought you filled that position already."

"Oh, we did. That's the one we're looking for."

••••••••••••

The insurance adjuster finished looking over the smoldering ruins of the warehouse fire. The warehouse owner had been following the man on his inspection.

"Well, what do you think caused the fire?" said the owner.

"It is a clear case of friction."

"Friction," said the owner. "I don't understand."

"The fire was started by rubbing a half-million-dollar insurance policy against a $400,000 warehouse!"

"Art department make the coffee again?"

"Dad, the bank you told me to put my money into seems to be in really bad financial shape," said Henry.

"Why, that doesn't seem possible. I know several of their directors and they tell me the bank has assets in the billions."

"Well, it's not true, Dad. Today one of my checks came back stamped 'insufficient funds.'"

• • • • • • • • • • •

"Miss Betencourt, when you were hired you told us you had five years' experience with computers and word processing. I don't think you've ever been in front of a computer before."

"Well, your ad said you wanted someone with imagination!"

• • • • • • • • • • •

Two bond brokers were talking.

"Did you know that Noah was the greatest financier who ever lived?"

"How do you figure?"

"He was able to float a company when the whole world was in liquidation!"

• • • • • • • • • • •

A stock broker was on vacation in Bermuda when he became violently ill and was rushed by ambulance to the Hamilton hospital. He came out of a coma just as a nurse was removing a thermometer from under his tongue.

"Do I have a temperature, nurse?" he said weakly.

"Yes, you do. A hundred and two."

The broker closed his eyes. "When it gets to a hundred and three, sell."

• • • • • • • • • • •

The computer salesman was showing the businessman a new machine.

"With the executive software program loaded into this computer, it will cut your secretary's work load in half."

"Good. I'll take two."

• • • • • • • • • • •

The supervisor tapped the typist on the shoulder and gestured to the sign on the wall.

"Can't you see that the sign says no smoking while you're working."

"Who says I'm working?"

• • • • • • • • • • •

The manager sent a fax to his major supplier:

MOVE HEAVEN AND EARTH.
NEED SHIPMENT BY FRIDAY.

The manufacturer faxed back the next day:

HAVE RAISED HELL.
SHIPMENT THERE BY THURSDAY.

• • • • • • • • • • •

At the end of his first day on the job, Wilson was ambling toward his car to head home when his boss stopped him.

"Wilson, we won't need you tomorrow. Here's your pay for loafing seven hours on the job."

"Excuse me, Mr. Benson, it was eight hours!"

• • • • • • • • • • •

Henderson knocked on the boss's door.

"Mr. Johnson, I'd like to talk to you about a raise. I really feel I deserve one and I've been praying for one in church every Sunday."

"Henderson, what did I tell you about going over my head!"

• • • • • • • • • • •

He was a self-made man who owed his lack of success to nobody.

Joseph Heller

• • • • • • • • • • •

"Miss Fargis, would you come into my office for a minute?" said the supervisor. He then closed the door.

"Mr. Simpson said that you called him a male sexist pig."

"That's about right."

"He also said that you called him a lazy, good-for-nothing son of a bitch."

"Pretty close to what I said."

"He also alleges that you called him a cheap, two-bit gold-bricking, lying sack of good-for-nothing trash."

Fargis thought for a moment. "No I didn't, but if you'll repeat that slowly I'll write it down!"

• • • • • • • • • • • •

Punctuality is one of the cardinal business virtues: Always insist on it in your subordinates.

Don Marquis

• • • • • • • • • • • •

Thelma, the office manager's wife, was in town shopping and stopped into the office. Her husband was on the phone as she came in and she tiptoed up behind him, put her hands over his eyes, and leaned her face next to his ear.

"Guess who?" she cooed.

"I told you we had no time to fool around," her husband bellowed. "Now get those letters out!"

• • • • • • • • • • •

A husband burst in while his wife was watching television.

"I just found a great job. Thirty-five hours a week, three-week paid vacation, benefits, and only ten minutes from home!"

"That's just wonderful, dear," said his wife munching on a bonbon.

"I knew you'd be excited, honey. You start Monday."

• • • • • • • • • • •

People who work sitting down get paid more than people who work standing up.

Ogden Nash

• • • • • • • • • • •

Mr. Bresnick, an American businessman, was on holiday in Israel. He had filled his seven-day vacation by seeing every sight and landmark in the country. Tired out but satisfied, he hailed a cab for the airport.

"So how was your stay in the country?" asked the taxi driver.

"Terrific," replied Mr. Bresnick. "I saw everything." And he proceeded to run down his itinerary.

"Very complete," said the cab driver. "But you didn't see one of our most famous sights, the statue of the unknown soldier."

"I've never heard of that one," remarked the tourist. "I've got several hours before my flight. Can we see it?"

With that the driver turned and headed through traffic. Soon they stopped in front of a magnificent 100-foot-high statue of a soldier standing with a rifle. A large brass plaque at the foot of the statue read:

SAM SCHWARTZ, BELOVED HUSBAND OF SADIE, FATHER OF ZEV AND ARIE.

BORN IN RIGA, POLAND, SEPTEMBER 14, 1909. ISRAEL'S UNKNOWN SOLDIER.

"Very impressive." remarked Mr. Bresnick after several minutes. "But I don't understand. The plaque lists his wife, his children, when he was born. How can he be an unknown soldier?"

The cab driver shrugged. "As a soldier, he was unknown. But as an accountant… "

••••••••••••

If only God would give me some clear sign! Like making a deposit in my name in a Swiss bank account.

Woody Allen

••••••••••••

Harry sat down at the table in the company cafeteria. He unloaded his tray, then squeezed a half a lemon into a glass of iced tea, and took a sip.

"Not tart enough," he grumbled. "And this is the last piece of lemon they had."

The large man sitting opposite Harry leaned over and took the half-squeezed lemon and crushed it in his powerful fist. Several teaspoons of lemon juice trickled down into the glass.

"Impressive," admired Harry. "Where do you work?"

"Warehouse," said the man. "And I work out every day besides."

Harry took another swallow and shook his head. "Still too sweet."

A little man with receding hair who had been listening asked if he might help. Harry nodded and the man picked up the limp lemon, made a tiny fist, and squeezed. A good pint of lemon juice gushed forth.

Harry was astonished. "Where do you work?"

"Accounts Collectible."

• • • • • • • • • • • •

It is well known what a middleman is: He is a man who bamboozles one party and plunders the other.

Benjamin Disraeli

• • • • • • • • • • • •

An oil prospector died and was met by St. Peter at the Heavenly Gates.

"I have bad news," said St. Peter, walking along with the prospector. "You're certainly qualified for residence here in Heaven, but there's no room to squeeze you in." St. Peter waved to a crowded hill behind a gate. "As you can see, the section reserved for oil men is full."

The prospector thought for a moment and then asked if he might just say just four words to the present occupants. St. Peter agreed to the proposition. The prospector cupped his hands and yelled "Oil discovered in Hell!" In a split second the gate opened and the compound emptied as all the oil men scrambled to be the first down to Hell.

St. Peter, amazed, invited the prospector to move right in.

The prospector shook his head and headed for the Gate. "No," he said, "I think I'll go along with the rest of them. There might be some truth to that rumor."

••••••••••••

By working faithfully eight hours a day, you may eventually get to be a boss and work twelve hours a day.

Robert Frost

Paula returned to her desk after a closed-door meeting with her boss

"Paula, how did your six-month review go? Does he like the job you're doing?" asked Vickie.

"Well, he didn't exactly say I was doing a good job. He said I'm the least of his worries."

Robinson Crusoe started the forty-hour week. He had all his work done by Friday.

Leopold Fechtner

A man met with his accountant. "How much is five hundred plus five hundred?" asked the man.

Replied the cooperative accountant, "What number did you have in mind?"

The assistant was extolling the virtues of her friend to the company president who was looking to fill an opening in the training program.

"Kevin went to Hotchkiss, then he did his undergraduate work at Princeton. He was at Cambridge for two years studying international trade, then he came back and went to UVA for a year for business. Then he went… "

"Miss Thornton," interrupted her boss. "It's a program for training managers, not for breeding them."

Committee: A group of men who keep minutes and waste hours.

Milton Berle

"And how much does the position pay?" asked the prospective employee.

"A hundred and twenty-five dollars a week."

"What! I'd be insulted to work for that low a weekly salary."

"Don't worry. We pay it every two weeks. That way you'll be insulted less often!"

• • • • • • • • • • •

Lee, a company president, arrived home after a stormy director's meeting.

His wife met him at the door with a martini, which Lee immediately gulped down. Catching his breath, he turned to his wife.

"It was a rough meeting. The company is not doing well and we will have to cut back on a number of luxuries at home. If you would learn to cook, we could fire the chef."

His wife laughed. "If you could learn to make love, we could fire the chauffeur."

• • • • • • • • • • •

Q. How many creative directors does it take to screw in a light bulb?

A. Does it have to be a light bulb?

•••••••••••••

Adam and Eve were the first bookkeepers because they invented the loose-leaf system.

•••••••••••

"Do you have anything to say before I fire you, Terwilliger?"

"Yes. Can I have a raise?"

•••••••••••

If you get to 35 and your job still involves wearing a name tag, you've probably made a serious vocational error.

Dennis Miller

•••••••••••

Bob met his friend Steve on the elevator.

"Bob, with all the cutbacks, how's it going in your department? Is your job in jeopardy?"

"No, my job is secure. It's me they want to lay off."

Fitzgerald, the new young assistant, poked his head into his boss's office.

"Is it okay if I take the afternoon off?" he asked. "My wife is having a baby."

His boss was understanding and gestured him out, "Of course, go on home."

The next day the assistant was back at his desk working. His boss spotted him and rushed up.

"Well, did she have a boy or a girl?" she asked excitedly.

"Oh, it's too soon to tell," Fitzgerald answered. "We'll have to wait nine months to find out."

I have enough money to last the rest of my life, unless I buy something.

Jackie Mason

•••••••••••

The salesman greeted his friend as the latter strolled into the hotel bar.

"How'd it go today, Ben?"

"Real good, Jack. I made some really fine business contacts that will prove to be extremely valuable."

Jack took a swallow of beer. "Yeah, I didn't make any sales today either!"

•••••••••••

Wall Street: A thoroughfare that begins in a graveyard and ends in a river.

Anonymous

•••••••••••

Harry worked till eight at the office. Finally finishing the report, he offered to take his hard-working and beautiful assistant to dinner. After a sumptuous meal, a bottle of wine, the two ended up at the assistant's apartment for a nightcap. One thing led to another and soon they were in the bedroom rolling around on the bed. Hours later, Harry got back into his clothes and before leaving asked his assistant for a piece of chalk which he stuck behind his ear.

Arriving home at three in the morning, he tiptoed in to find his wife at the top of the stairs.

"And just where have you been to this hour," she demanded.

"I worked late at the office, then my assistant and I had dinner and went back to her apartment where we made love for hours."

"Liar! I see that chalk behind your ear. You've been out playing pool!"

• • • • • • • • • • • •

Q. How many software programmers does it take to screw in a light bulb?

A. None. It's a hardware problem.

•••••••••••

"You say you worked ten years at Kennedy's," said the personnel manager to the applicant. "But on your personnel form you list the years 1988 to 1992. That's not ten years."

"You've never worked for Bill Kennedy!"

•••••••••••

Bryant, a businessman, traveled to Kenya for a long-awaited safari trip. Just a day after the safari group set out, Bryant was separated from the rest of his party, and soon was hopelessly lost. With no gun and just a Swiss Army knife, he hacked out a crude hut of leaves and waited patiently for a rescue party.

Weeks went by with no sign of a search party. Finally there came a knock on the grass flap of his hut.

Bryant slowly raised himself off the ground. "Who is it?" he asked weakly.

"The Red Cross."

"I gave at the office."

•••••••••••

The trouble with unemployment is that the minute you wake up you're on the job.

Slappy White

•••••••••••

Elliot finished his coffee at the counter and asked the waitress if he might use the phone. When the other party answered, he spoke.

"Hello, I'm calling about an ad you placed in the newspaper about two months ago for an executive assistant. Has the job been filled?"

"Oh, yes. We hired someone about six weeks ago and he is excellent."

After Elliot had hung up, the waitress looked at him quizzically.

"I thought you had a new job," she asked. "What are you calling another company for?"

"Oh no, you misunderstand," replied Elliot. "That was my new boss. I just wanted to see if I was still doing a good job."

•••••••••••

Kavanagh, the union official, emerged from the closed-door meeting with the auto company officials. It had been tough round-the-clock bargaining, but after four weeks an agreement had been hammered out.

"Here are the details of the agreement," announced the official to the workers gathered in the union hall. "For senior members, the yearly salary is $50,000 plus free medical and dental, retirement at age 44, mileage to and from the plant, car insurance paid for, all college costs for your kids paid for, and you only have to come to the plant on Fridays."

"Hey, Kavanagh," groused one member, "is that every Friday?"

•••••••••••

Florence, a new employee, was twenty minutes late getting to the office, an improvement over yesterday's arrival when she was a half-hour late and the day before, when she was forty minutes tardy. She was just sitting down at her desk when the boss walked over.

"Miss Brown, do you have any idea when we start work here?"

"How could I, Mr. Layden. Everybody's always working by the time I get here!"

"You'll find I run this place just like a democracy. Only nobody votes."

• • • • • • • • • • •

"How's business, Paul?"

"Couldn't be better," Paul answered. "I sleep like a baby."

"Really?"

"Yeah, I wake up every two hours and cry!"

• • • • • • • • • • •

Q. What does an accountant do when he's constipated?

A. Works it out with a pencil.

• • • • • • • • • • •

The president's secretary buzzed his office and said that a Mr. Pierce, the head of an employment agency, was on the phone. He picked up the receiver.

"Yes, this is Mr. Simpson. What can I do for you?"

"We have a client who has listed your company on his resume and we'd like to confirm a few facts," said Mr. Pierce.

"Okay. What's the name of this person?"

"His name is Gene Minoff and he says that he worked for you as a salesman."

"Yes, he did," responded Simpson, "for about two weeks."

"Two weeks!" exclaimed Pierce. "He says he was employed by you for four years."

"That's right."

• • • • • • • • • • •

Money: The only substance which can keep a cold world from nicknaming a citizen "Hey you!"

Wilson Mizner

• • • • • • • • • • •

A junior partner in the firm walked into the senior vice-president's office. He slumped into a chair, downhearted, disconsolate, his head hanging down.

"Sid, what's the matter. I've never seen you so down."

"Bart, I don't know what to do," Sid breathed

heavily. "I'm about to be audited by the IRS and I'm completely bewildered. I don't know how to approach it. I've talked to my accountant and my brother-in-law and they've given me conflicting advice."

"What did they tell you?"

"First, my brother-in-law said to go to a used clothing store and buy a ratty old suit of clothes, a shirt with a frayed collar, and an old stained tie. Then he told me to get a beat up pair of shoes and rent an old jalopy. I'm supposed to drive down to the IRS office, park in front and walk in for the meeting. Then throw myself on their mercy and see what they say."

The senior officer leaned forward. "What did your accountant tell you to do?"

"He told me to go to Brooks Brothers and pick out a fifteen-hundred-dollar suit. Buy a nice Turnbull & Asser shirt, a Sulka tie, and go out and rent the longest limousine I can find. Finally, I should get a business card from a partner in the most impressive law firm in the city, go down in the limo and park in front of the IRS office. Then walk in and slap the card on the desk and say, 'If I get called about this matter one more time you'll be hearing from my lawyer.'"

Sid sighed, "So you can see, Bart, I don't know which to do. What do you think?"

Bart paused for a moment before replying.

"Sid, let me tell you about a young secretary who was in here yesterday with a problem. She's getting married next week and came to me for some advice. 'Mr. Harrison,' she said, 'I don't know what to wear on my wedding night. My sister said that when my husband and I are together in the bedroom for the first time I should come out of the dressing room wearing a white, cotton, floor-length nightgown with a high collar and long sleeves, and I should be wearing white cotton panties underneath.

"'Then my girl friend said something quite different. She told me to come out of the dressing room wearing a sheer, black, sleeveless, waist-length negligee cut down to the navel, with black lace peekaboo panties underneath.'"

Sid was curious. "So, Bart, what advice did you give her?"

"I gave her the same advice I'm going to give you, Sid," Bart answered, leaning forward. "It doesn't matter what you wear. Either way you're going to get screwed!"

•••••••••••

The telephone kept ringing until finally the executive looked up from his budget calculations and yelled, "Miss Smootley, will you answer the damn phone?"

"Why should I. It's always for you."

•••••••••••

Frank Hoffman, a business executive, died and arrived at the Heavenly Gates to meet St. Peter.

"I see from your records," St. Peter intoned, "that you've led a decent life. In this day and age, that entitles you to a choice between Heaven and Hell. But I'm sure you'll choose us after you take the tour."

Then St. Peter took Hoffman on a walk around Heaven. Green hills, waterfalls, gardens, lush golf courses, and clear skies greeted them on their stroll.

"Beautiful, isn't it?" beamed St. Peter. "Now I'll take you back to the Gates where you can catch an elevator to Hell."

"There you are," said the Devil to Frank as they

stepped into the elevator. "Ready for the tour?"

Moments later the elevator arrived at the bottom stop and the doors opened. Beautiful men and gorgeous women frolicked in several large swimming pools next to a tree-shaded clubhouse. Waiters scurried about with huge platters of food, buckets of champagne, and frozen drinks for people clad in designer outfits.

"Why, it looks like a country club," exclaimed Hoffman as he looked around.

The next day Hoffman stood in front of St. Peter and the Devil at the Heavenly Gates. "I've made up my mind," he said. "I'm taking Hell."

When the elevator doors opened they were greeted by a blast of hot air. Hoffman peered out into a fiery cavern as perspiring workers struggled to stoke furnaces. He turned to the Devil in anger. "What's going on? This is nothing like what you showed me yesterday!?"

The Devil smiled wickedly. "Ah, but yesterday you were a prospect. Today you're a client!"

• • • • • • • • • • • •

The company's human resources manager received a fat envelope from the government. Inside were extensive forms to be filled out in triplicate with a list of all employees broken down by sex. The manager put the forms on a corner of his desk where they were quickly buried by more pressing matters. A month later, a stern letter arrived from the same government department warning him to fill out the form.

He soon uncovered the forms and scrawled across the front: "We have no employees broken down by sex. They get broken down by alcohol."

• • • • • • • • • • • •

The manager of the department store watched his new employee count the register receipts at closing time. The employee was very fast and finished counting the money ahead of everyone else.

Liking what he saw, the manager walked over and asked the employee where he had gotten his training.

"Yale," the new employee answered.

"Impressive," answered the manager. "And what is your name?"

"Yim Yackson."

• • • • • • • • • • • •

You know, if an orange and an apple went into conference consultations, it might come out a pear.

Ronald Reagan

•••••••••••

Two businessmen were riding the 8:07 together from Croton when one looked up from his newspaper and said, "My son just graduated from college and has gone into business for himself."

"That's good news," offered his friend.

"Good news and bad news," the man countered

"What's the good news?" the friend asked.

"He opened a submarine shop."

"What's the bad news?"

"He went under."

•••••••••••

The boss was visiting the Dallas office, and he and the branch manager were walking past the rows of desks.

"Say, Aaron, what happened to those 'Think' signs I asked you to put up on all the walls?"

"I had to take them down, Mr. Pyke. Everyone sat around thinking and we didn't get any work done."

•••••••••••

One of my first office jobs was cleaning the windows on the envelopes.

Rita Rudner

•••••••••••

The salesman walked into the sporting goods store to see the buyer. He opened his sample case to display reels, fishing rods, line, and lures. After handing over a fistful of catalogs to the buyer, he reached in his case and pulled out a neon-colored lure that was blinking on and off.

"Newest and best lure in the business," he assured the buyer. "Runs on a hearing aid battery that keeps it flashing for hours."

The buyer was not convinced. "Do you really sell a lot of them? I can't believe a bass would go for this thing."

The salesman grinned. "Of course we've shipped a lot of them! We don't sell them to the fish; we sell them to the suckers."

• • • • • • • • • • •

Money does not necessarily bring happiness. People with twenty million dollars are no happier than people with ten million.

Jim Charlton

• • • • • • • • • • •

Glenn, a businessman, was frequently out of the office playing golf. He carefully instructed his long-time secretary to tell anyone who called that he was away from his desk, and that he would get back to them. Which he did—from the clubhouse.

One day, after he had left the office, his golf partner, who had forgotten which of two golf courses they were supposed to play that day, called Glenn's office to find out. Glenn's loyal secretary kept repeating that Glenn was away from his desk and would get back to him.

Exasperated at the secretary's stonewalling, the partner finally yelled into the phone, "Just tell me, is he ten miles away from his desk or twenty miles?"

• • • • • • • • • • • •

Corporation: An ingenious device for obtaining individual profit without individual responsibility.

Ambrose Bierce

• • • • • • • • • • • •

As Dan was teeing his ball up, he turned to his partner and asked, "Do you know why golf is like taxes?"

"No."

You drive hard to get to the green and then you end up in the hole!"

• • • • • • • • • • • •

Art Harrison, a businessman, and his attractive young assistant, Laurie, flew to New York City for an important meeting, scheduled the following afternoon with a big client. When they arrived in the evening at the hotel, they were informed that somehow their reservation had been misdirected and there was nothing booked in their names.

Furthermore, because of the electronics convention in town, all the hotels were filled. Harrison pulled the manager aside and finally prevailed upon him to find them one small room that he and Laurie could share. He asked Laurie if, under the circumstances, she minded. Laurie said no.

After the two had unpacked, gotten into their night clothes and climbed into bed, they were finally getting comfortable. Then Laurie raised her head and said, "Mr. Harrison, would you close the window. It's cold in here."

Harrison opened his eyes. "Would you like to pretend that we're married, Laurie?"

"Oh, yes, Mr. Harrison," she breathed softly.

"Then close the damn window yourself!"

• • • • • • • • • • • •

Mr. Cathers finished dictating the letter to his secretary and taking his feet off the desk asked, "Did I go too fast for you, Miss Brown?"

"Oh, I got it all, Mr. Cathers. Do you want me to leave the grammatical errors in or out?"

••••••••••••

The two commodity brokers, Harris and White, were in an auto accident and woke up the next morning in adjoining beds in the hospital. The attending physician was making his rounds, and pulled the chair up next to Harris.

Somberly and quietly he said, "Mr. Harris, I've got some good news and some bad news for you. Which do you want first?"

"Give me the bad news."

"I have to amputate both your legs."

"Oh my God," gasped Harris, "What's the good news."

"Mr. White wants to buy your slippers."

••••••••••••

At the DMMA convention, two rival executives found themselves in adjoining urinals in the men's room. They finished at the same time. One went over to wash his hands, while the other headed for the door.

The man washing his hands looked up and said, "At Wharton we were taught to wash our hands after pissing."

The other executive sneered, "At the B School we were taught not to piss on our hands."

•••••••••••

There were times my pants were so thin that I could sit on a dime and tell if it were heads or tails.

Spencer Tracy

•••••••••••

The two business partners hired a new secretary, a beautiful, curvaceous blond, 22-year-old. Both partners were smitten with her and both starting seeing her after work hours. Inevitably, she got pregnant.

When her condition was apparent, the two partners decided that the best thing for all concerned was to send her to Florida to have the baby, and they would pay all her expenses. Finally, in her sixth month, she departed for Miami. Several months went by without a word from her, and by this point, the partners became worried. One decided that he would combine a business trip to Florida with seeing the young lady.

His first night there, he called his partner from the hotel.

"How is she, Sam?" inquired the partner.

"She's fine, Ben. But I've got some good news and some bad news."

"What's the good news?" asked Sam.

"The good news is that she's fine, she's healthy, and she's had twins."

"Wow, that's incredible, " exclaimed Sam. "What's the bad news?"

"Mine died."

• • • • • • • • • • • •

In the newspaper was an ad listing a job opening in the office of an international trading company. The requirements were that the person be able to type, take dictation, be familiar with computers, and speak more than one language.

The first applicant for the job was a dog. The personnel manager was skeptical but, being in an equal opportunity office, she proceeded with the interview. The dog sat at a typewriter and immediately zipped through the typing test at 125 words per minute. The dog next took errorless dictation, then proceeded to the computer in the office and whipped through various spread sheets, word programs, and software.

The manager was amazed. She had never seen anyone as proficient as the fuzzy, brown-and-white applicant. "You are really the most qualified individual we've had in here in quite a while!" she said admiringly. "Now for the last requirement on the job— the second language."

The dog hesitated and then looked up. "Meow!"

••••••••••••

It was pitch black and the wind was howling when the traveling salesman saw the farmhouse. He parked in the driveway and knocked on the front door. When the farmer opened the door, the salesman asked him if he had a extra bed where he might sleep for the night.

"We're cramped for space, mister," said the farmer, "so I'll have to put you in with my three sons."

"Excuse me," replied the salesman, backing out, "I must be in the wrong joke."

• • • • • • • • • • •

Q. How many conservative economists does it take to screw in a light bulb?

A. None. They let the market do it.

• • • • • • • • • • •

"Isn't she beautiful?" said the first Martian, looking at the lap-top computer. "I think I'll take her back to Mars."

"Watch out," said the other Martian. "She looks underage."

• • • • • • • • • • •

There are worse things in life than death. Have you ever spent an evening with an insurance salesman?

Woody Allen

"His phone is busy, his fax is busy and his modem is busy. I'll just walk over and talk to him."

• • • • • • • • • • • •

Art, the stock broker, phoned his client. "I got an inside tip on National Uranium and I think you should take a strong position. It's at $10 a share."

"Thanks, Art," said the client. "Let's buy 20,000 shares."

The next day the stock rose to $11 a share. Art phoned his client again. "Do you want to sell?"

"Sell? Buy another 20,000 shares."

By Friday the stock opened at $15 a share. This time the client phoned Art. "None of this selling stuff. Buy another 20,000 shares!"

By midday though, disaster had struck and the stock plunged to $7 a share. "Sell me out!" cried the client.

"To whom?"

• • • • • • • • • • • •

Two advertising agency executives were having lunch and gossiping about the agency business.

"Where is Lee Simons these days?" the first one asked.

"Didn't you hear? Lee got sick and died. He went to that big agency in the sky."

"That's terrible!" gasped the first executive. "What did he have?"

"Not much," said the second. "Couple of publishers, a tooth paste account, and a bank. Nothing worth going after."

• • • • • • • • • • • •

The young man finished his monologue to his boss about why he deserved a salary raise. His boss listened without interruption until the man had finished.

"Harry, I know you can't get married on the salary I'm paying you. And some day you'll thank me for that!"

• • • • • • • • • • • •

Two former college roommates met to have drinks.

"So how's the stock brokerage business?" the first asked.

"Well, it's sort of like sex," the broker answered. "When it's good, it's wonderful—and when it's bad, it's still pretty good!"

Q. How many bankers does it take to screw in a light bulb?

A. Four. One to hold the light bulb and three to try and remember the combination.

• • • • • • • • • • •

Corporate vice-president: One who takes the padding out of shoulders and puts it on his expense account.

• • • • • • • • • • •

Cooper, the associate vice-president of the bank, was an aging but still dangerous sexist. He had terrorized generations of pretty, young secretaries and assistants with his pinching, groping, and lewd remarks. Now almost seventy, he was a month away from retirement.

That Monday morning his failing eyes lit up when he saw a new secretary swish by his office door, her skirt cut a good four inches above the knees. But by the time Cooper had gotten out of his chair, maneuvered around his desk, and made it to the door, all he saw was the young woman turning the corner and disappearing.

A veteran secretary looked up from her desk and nudged the woman at the next desk.

"Look at poor Cooper. His eyes are on their last legs!"

•••••••••••

To err is human but to really foul up requires a computer.

Paul Erlich

•••••••••••

Two partners in the garment district in New York had had a great year. Their entire line sold out with reorders, back orders, and spring orders for everything they made. With everything in great shape, one of the partners took a well-earned vacation to the Bahamas. He had only been gone two days when he got a frantic phone call from his partner.

"Roger, Roger, something terrible has happened. Our safe has been robbed and $100,000 is gone."

"Mort," his partner replied calmly, "that's going too far. Put $90,000 back in the safe!"

• • • • • • • • • • •

Saul Stine was a tough businessman and was infamous for always postdating his checks to creditors. When he died, his creditors got their revenge. Over Saul's grave, they erected a tombstone that read:

HERE LIES SAUL STINE.
DIED AUGUST 15, AS OF OCTOBER 10.

• • • • • • • • • • •

The phone rang and Beckett picked it up.

"Mr. Beckett, this is Ed Dawson. I'm calling to see if you got the check we sent you."

"Yes I did. Twice."

"Twice?"

"Yes, once from you and once from the bank!"

• • • • • • • • • • •

The two businessmen met on the street.

"How's business?" asked the first.

"Well, it's a non-profit organization, you know."

"No, I didn't know that was your business," replied the first.

"Neither did I till I found out I couldn't make a profit."

• • • • • • • • • • • •

The two businessmen, Walker and Goldstein, were out fishing off the coast of Connecticut. It was a clear day when the two set out, and when the fish started biting the men failed to notice a huge storm approaching. Suddenly thunder and lightning hit, rain came pelting down, and giant waves pounded the boat. Seconds later, a huge wave capsized the boat and Walker and Goldstein were thrown in the roiling water.

"Goldstein, are you all right?" sputtered Walker as he flailed in the surf.

"I'm okay," cried Goldstein. "Let's try and swim to shore."

"It's too far to swim," yelled Walker. "We'll never make it. Try and float. O.K.?"

"I hear you," gasped Goldstein. "But can you float alone?"

"Goldstein!" barked Walker. "Is this a time to talk business?!"

• • • • • • • • • • •

Q. How many office managers does it take to screw in a light bulb?

A. Seventy-seven. One to notice the burned-out bulb, his supervisor to authorize a requisition, a typist to fill out the requisition, four clerks to file requisition copies, a delivery person to take the requisition to the purchasing department, a mail order clerk to pick up the requisition form and take it to her department....

• • • • • • • • • • •

"Betty, how long have you been working here?" asked the new employee.

"Ever since the boss threatened to fire me."

• • • • • • • • • • •

Benny Carter owned a hot dog stand that he parked every day at the corner of 52nd and 6th Avenue. One day one of his regular customers asked Benny how he was doing.

"Terrific!" Benny answered. "In two years I've put $10,000 into the bank."

The man was impressed. "Well, Benny, maybe you'd loan me a hundred?"

"I'd like to but I can't," said Benny emphatically.

"You can't?"

"No, I've got this agreement with the bank. They won't sell hot dogs and I won't loan money."

• • • • • • • • • • •

The four deliverymen slowly wheeled the new mainframe computer into the building lobby and pushed it to the delivery elevator. There they were stopped.

"Harry, it's too big for the elevator. How are we going to get it to the ninth floor?"

Harry mopped his brow. "Let's plug the damn thing in and let the computer figure it out."

• • • • • • • • • • •

Julio knocked tentatively on the office door of his boss, a steely, blond, humorless woman named Burke.

"Yes, Julio, what is it? I'm busy."

"Yes, Ms. Burke. It'll just take a minute." He slithered into a chair. "You see, I haven't had a raise in three years, though you promised me one when I first arrived. I work over fifty hours a week. I do everything you ask. And since I've been here, I've gotten married and have two children to feed. How about fifty dollars a week more?"

"Julio, you're right," said Ms. Burke after a moment. "You've got it."

An ecstatic Julio rushed home on Friday with his increased paycheck to show his wife. The following Friday arrived and Julio looked in his pay envelope to find his salary back to the old number. Once again, he went down the hall and knocked on his boss's door. When he was invited in he quickly blurted out, "Ms. Burke, what happened to my $50 raise?"

"You mean you wanted it every week?"

• • • • • • • • • • • •

My problem lies in reconciling my gross habits with my net income.

Errol Flynn

• • • • • • • • • • •

Henry Reath, the assistant vice-president at the insurance company, was frustrated after being passed over for promotion time and again. Desperate to try anything, he checked in to Johns Hopkins for a new and risky procedure, a brain transplant. After a battery of tests, he was accepted into the program.

"Doctor, I know the risks in the operation," said Henry, "but what is the actual cost?"

"It is not inexpensive," answered the doctor, "and it depends on the brain we use. For instance, an ounce of brain from a CPA costs $2,000, an ounce from a lawyer costs $5,000, while an ounce from an ad executive's brain costs $75,000."

"$75,000 an ounce!" exclaimed Henry. "Why so high, doctor?"

"Do you realize how many ad executives we have to kill?!"

• • • • • • • • • • •

Smith complained that he was a two-handicap golfer. His boss won't let him off early and his wife keeps him home on the weekends.

• • • • • • • • • • •

Consultant: Any ordinary guy more than fifty miles from home.

Eric Sevareid

• • • • • • • • • • •

Q. How many corporate vice-presidents does it take to screw in a light bulb?

A. Two. One to screw it in. One to screw it up.

• • • • • • • • • • •

The two clothing salesmen were having lunch and discussing business.

"Boy, did I have a great day yesterday," said the first. "I had a two-million-dollar order from the Supercheap stores."

"Two million!" scoffed the other. "I don't believe you."

"You don't believe me?" responded the first. "I'll show you the canceled order to prove it!"

••••••••••••

The man stomped into the bank and pushed his way through the queue to the cashier's window.

"I want to open a goddam checking account," he snarled.

The cashier looked up from his counting. "I beg your pardon?"

"Open your goddam ears. I said I want to open a goddam checking account."

He looked at him disapprovingly. "I'm sorry, this is a respectable establishment. We don't allow that sort of language in here." With that, he slammed down the gate on his window.

The bank president, hearing the ruckus, rushed over. "Here, here, sir. What is the meaning of all this commotion going on?"

The man turned to the executive. "I just won a goddam five million dollars in the goddam lottery and I want to open a goddam checking account."

The bank president smiled. "And is this bastard giving you a hard time?"

"Miss Kavell, when's the last time I stopped to smell the flowers?"

• • • • • • • • • • •

"I hate this new computer!" complained the secretary. "It never does what I want it to do; only what I tell it!"

• • • • • • • • • • •

The IRS has proposed a new and simplified short tax form that they believe will be fair to everyone. It consists of just two lines:

1) How much money did you make last year?

$____________

2) Send it in.

• • • • • • • • • • •

"Miss Smith, you write here on your application that the reason you left your last job was 'sickness.' Are you over your illness?"

"Oh, I wasn't sick, it was my boss."

"Your boss?"

"Yeah, she was sick of me!"

•••••••••••

Q. What's the difference between a pigeon and a stockbroker?

A. In this economy a pigeon can still make a deposit on a BMW.

•••••••••••

The first Rotarian was the first man to call John the Baptist, Jack.

H. L. Mencken

•••••••••••

Three friends had drinks together a couple of times a week after work. This had been going on regularly for years until one day Charley arrived agitated and said he had a confession to make to the other two.

"Since I was young I've sensed that I was really a woman trapped in a man's body. And now I'm going to do something about it. I'm leaving tomorrow for Europe to have a sex-change operation and I'll be gone for twelve months."

Charley then shook hands with his astonished friends and left.

Exactly a year later, the two friends were having drinks in the same bar when a lovely looking, buxom blond strode into the bar and sat down on the empty stool next to the two.

"Hi fellas, remember me?"

The two gaped for several moments before one of them stammered, "Ch, Charley?"

"It's Charlene now. Can I buy you guys a drink?"

Soon they were discussing the transformation of Charley over the past year.

"It must have really been painful, Charlene. All those operations. God, cutting off your penis must have been the worst!"

"No, not really," replied Charlene.

"Probably cutting off your balls was even more painful," winced the other friend.

"That hurt pretty much," agreed Charlene. "But it wasn't the most painful."

"What was then?" chorused the two.

"Getting my salary cut in half!"

•••••••••••

The brain is a wonderful organ; it starts working the moment you get up in the morning and doesn't stop until you get into the office.

Robert Frost

•••••••••••

"McIntosh, here's a key to the executive washroom."

"Gee, Mr. Thompson, thanks!"

"Mr. Benson arrives at two. Have it cleaned by then."

•••••••••••

The two businessmen met on the street.

The first asked, "How's business?"

The second man proceeded to give him a ten-minute rundown about inventory, bad debts, new customers, cash flow, and the state of the business.

He was still going on when the first man put his

hand up and interrupted, "Aren't you going to ask me about my business?"

"Oh, I'm sorry to run on like that. How is your business?"

"Ach, don't ask!"

••••••••••••

The office manager was suspicious that one of his clerks was stealing funds from the company. The clerk lived in a penthouse in the best part of Chicago, drove to work in a Ferrari, and lavishly spent money on meals and entertainment. While he couldn't prove anything, his suspicions finally got to be too much and he confronted the young clerk.

"Rochelle, you make $200 a week here and yet you live like the president of the company. I can't find any funds that you've absconded with, so where do you get this money?"

Rochelle explained that each week she raffled off 2,000 tickets at $1 apiece to friends and fellow employees.

"A raffle, huh!" exclaimed her boss. "What do you raffle off?"

"My pay check!"

••••••••••••

Not many Americans have been around the world, but their money sure has.

Walter Slezak

••••••••••••

The middle-aged pilot, laid off by his failing airline, applied for a job with a computer company. After filling out all the forms he waited to be interviewed by the personnel director. Finally he was ushered into her office.

She looked over the forms as the pilot sat in a chair. "I have a point that needs clarification on your medical form 3Z10. To the question 'When was the last time you had sex?' you put down 1955. Isn't that, er, a bit unusual?"

"Not really," answered the pilot looking at his watch. "It's only 2100 now!"

• • • • • • • • • • •

I am a friend of the working man, and I would rather be a friend than be one.

Clarence Darrow

• • • • • • • • • • •

A factory worker broke his legs while on the job, and sued his company claiming that he was crippled for life. At the trial, the insurance company assembled a number of medical experts who testified that the worker's legs had healed perfectly and there was absolutely nothing wrong with him. But the specter of the wheelchair-bound worker surrounded by his wife and children swayed the jury and they awarded him a three-million-dollar settlement.

The following week, the worker was wheeled into the office of the lawyer representing the insurance company. The lawyer, flanked by several insurance company executives, was still outraged at the court's decision.

"You'll never get away with this, Fitzgerald. We are going to have you and your family followed day and night. We'll spy on you wherever you go. We'll have cameras on you every minute and if you take one step out of that wheel chair, we'll haul you back in court so fast it'll make your head spin."

With that outburst, the lawyer handed over the certified check. "There's your money. What are you going to do with it?"

Fitzgerald looked with satisfaction at the check. "My wife and I are going to take a trip to Europe. London, Dublin, Barcelona, Paris, and finally Lourdes. And it's there, gentleman, that you are going to witness one of the great miracles of the 20th century!"

• • • • • • • • • • •

Q. How can you tell if the dumb secretary has been using the computer?

A. There's whiteout on the screen.

• • • • • • • • • • •

Morris, the 90-year-old grand patriarch of the retail business he had started, lay on his death bed.

Around him in hushed silence gathered his three sons, a number of grandchildren, daughters-in-law, and attendants. Slowly Morris opened his eyes and looked around.

"Harry," he gasped, and his eldest son quickly sprung to his side.

"Here, Dad," said Harry.

"Where's Robert?" wheezed Morris, referring to his middle son.

"Robert is right here." Harry reassured him.

"And what about Samuel? " Morris asked softly.

"On your other side, Dad."

Morris bolted up in bed. "Then who the hell is minding the store!"

• • • • • • • • • • •

At the end of the day Ozzie, a stockbroker, stuck his key in the door and dragged himself into his apartment. He poured himself a full glass of scotch and slumped into a chair. His wife came in from another room, and saw how depressed and distraught her husband was.

"Oz, what is it? What's the matter?"

Ozzie took a gulp of liquor. "It's the market," he rasped. "It plunged 500 points, all my stocks are down. I've lost a fortune. We'll have to sell everything. The cars, the house in the Hamptons, the paintings."

"Oh my god!" gasped his wife. She ran to an open window and leapt out, plunging down thirty stories to her death.

Ozzie took another sip and raised his eyes to the ceiling. "Thank you, Paine Webber."

• • • • • • • • • • • •

A well-dressed man drove his Rolls Royce into the bank parking lot and walked in to see the bank president.

"I'd like to borrow five thousand dollars for a month," said the man.

"Certainly," replied the official. "Since you don't have an account with us, is there some sort of collateral you can put up for the loan?"

The man pointed outside. "My car." Soon he had his money and the bank was in possession of his car.

A month later the man, now suntanned and relaxed, reentered the bank. He marched up to the bank president and plunked down $5,000 plus $50 interest. The official handed the man back his car keys and, then curious, asked him why he needed the loan.

"Oh, I didn't need the money," the man replied. "But where else could I park my Rolls for fifty bucks!"

• • • • • • • • • • • •

My formula for success? Rise early, work late, strike oil.

J. Paul Getty

• • • • • • • • • • • •

The genie of advertising suddenly appeared in the agency conference room and granted wishes to each of the three astonished men there: a copywriter, an art director, and an account executive.

The copywriter spoke first. "I'd like a great house on Cape Cod where I can finally write that novel I've always wanted to do. I want it to be a best-seller, get great reviews, and be an instant classic that they'll be teaching in college a hundred years from now."

The genie waved his wand and the copywriter disappeared.

The art director spoke next. "I want to go to Paris and live on the Left Bank with a beautiful model and finally do my paintings. I want them to be admired the world over and hung in the Metropolitan, the Louvre. Places like that."

The genie waved again and the art director disappeared. The genie then turned to the account exec and bowed. "Your wish is next."

"I want those two guys back here right now!"

• • • • • • • • • • • •

Q. How many General Motors employees does it take to screw in a light bulb?

A. A hundred. Ninety-nine to try and screw one in, and one to fire them all.

"Good morning, work load."

•••••••••••

That money talks
I'll not deny;
I heard it once:
It said, "Goodbye."

Richard Armour

•••••••••••

A man in Dallas walked into a savings and loan bank.

"I'm sorry, sir, we're closed," said the bank clerk.

"But your sign says 8 to 3," protested the man.

"Those are the odds that we'll be open tomorrow!"

•••••••••••

Saving is a very fine thing, especially when your parents have done it for you.

Winston Churchill

••••••••••••

Gilpen, a successful businessman, wanted his new son-in-law to come into the business as his eventual successor. He called the young man into his study.

"Paul, now that you're part of the family I'd like you to know that I plan on retiring soon and I'd like to give you fifty percent of my company as a wedding present."

"Thanks very much, Mr. Gilpen."

"You can start working in the factory, learn the assembly line, how the machinery works, the various functions... "

"Oh, I'd hate that, Mr. Gilpen. Can't stand the noise, the dust. No thanks."

"Then you can start in the front office. Learn how the sales projections are made, the statements, the balance sheets... "

"No, I hate paperwork and I can't stand to be confined in one space for too long."

"Well, what am I going to do with you, Paul? You won't work in the factory where we make all the products and you won't work in the front office where we manage it all."

"You could buy me out."

•••••••••••

Q. What do you get when you cross a lawyer and a godfather.

A. An offer you can't understand.

•••••••••••

I got a job as a short-order cook. I was cooking a chicken on the rotisserie, I was turning the wheel, and I was singing "Arrivederci, Roma," and a drunk came by and stopped. He said, "You got a nice voice but your monkey is on fire."

London Lee

•••••••••••

He had an office so tiny that one inch smaller and it would have been adultery.

Dorothy Parker

••••••••••••

A man, in town for an AFL-CIO convention, went looking for some action in the red-light district of the city. He went into the first house of ill repute he spotted and walked up to the madam.

"I'm looking for a good time and this looks like the right place for it." The woman nodded her assent. "But there's just one question, madam. I'm a lifetime union man and is this a union shop?" When she said no, he left.

This same scene was repeated several times along the street until he finally reached the last house on the block.

"Just one thing, madam. Is this a union shop?" When she said yes, a great big grin spread over his face, and he promptly paid her.

"Now I think I'll take that little blonde at the end of the couch," he said, pointing into the other room.

"No, you can't have her," said the proprietor. "Your date for the night is that one over there." She pointed out a little grey-haired lady in a shawl sitting in a chair.

"Her!" he protested. "Why don't I get my pick?"

"She has seniority."

•••••••••••

The art of taxation consists in so plucking the goose as to obtain the largest amount of feathers with the least amount of hissing.

Jean-Baptiste Colbert

•••••••••••

Two young women were walking through a meadow when they passed a large bullfrog. Suddenly the frog spoke.

"Kiss me, I'm an investment banker."

Without a moment's hesitation, one of the women reached down, picked the frog up, dropped him in her knapsack, and started walking on. The other woman looked at her.

"Aren't you going to kiss him and turn him back?"

"Are you kidding," sneered the first. "Investment bankers are a dime a dozen but a talking frog will make me a fortune!"

• • • • • • • • • • •

Two workers were washing up in the lavatory.

"Did you hear what happened to Kelly?" asked one.

"No."

"He was caught screwing around in the workroom with that blond secretary, Lorraine, and the boss fired him."

"That's terrible. What happened to Lorraine?"

"Nothing. She was on her lunch break."

• • • • • • • • • • •

Two retired businessmen were sitting beside the pool at a Miami condominium. They got to talking and discovered they were both from New York.

"What happened to your business, Mort?" asked the first.

"Fire destroyed it. And you?"

"Flood destroyed mine," answered Mort.

The first man thought for a minute before speaking.

"How do you start a flood?"

••••••••••••

Just before closing time at the Salisbury bank, two masked robbers burst in waving revolvers and demanded that all the employees take their clothes off and lay face down on the floor. All of the terrified employees complied as fast as they could. Betty, the most nervous of all, took off all her clothes and laid down on her back.

Ralph, a co-worker, looked over at her. "Betty," he hissed, "turn over. This isn't the office Christmas party!"

••••••••••••

The junk-bond dealer punched the button on his intercom.

"Masterson, get me my broker!"

"Yes sir," answered his secretary. "Stock or pawn?"

••••••••••••

Harry, a new employee at the company, got his first paycheck after two weeks. The check had a receipt where the employee signed showing he had received the money.

At the bottom of the receipt form was a notation that read: Your salary is your own business and should not be discussed with any of your fellow employees.

Harry initialed the receipt and then added: I won't mention it to a soul. I'm just as ashamed of it as you are.

• • • • • • • • • • • •

The clerk stood in front of his boss's desk shifting from one foot to the other. Finally, his boss looked up.

"Yes, Wilson, what is it?"

"I, er, ah," he stammered. "Could I use your phone?"

"What for?"

"To call my wife. She told me to ask you for a raise, but I can't remember how much she told me!"

• • • • • • • • • • • •

Beacom marched into his boss's office and pounded his fist on his desk.

"I'd like to tender my resignation."

"Don't make it tender, make it brief!"

• • • • • • • • • • • •

It is no secret that organized crime in America takes in over forty billion dollars a year. This is quite a profitable sum, especially when one considers that the Mafia spends very little for office supplies.

Woody Allen

• • • • • • • • • • • •

Salley, who had been working in the office for four years without a raise, finally screwed up his courage and walked into his boss's office.

"Madam, I've been working here without a raise for four years. I work eighty hours a week and do the work of three men. I deserve a raise."

His boss looked at him. "I can't give you a raise this year. But if you'll tell me who the other two men are, I'll have them fired!"

• • • • • • • • • • •

I'm living so far beyond my income that we might be said to be living apart.

Saki (H. H. Munro)

• • • • • • • • • • •

The customer followed the owner of the small dry goods store through his stockroom to the office. As they passed through the stockroom, the customer looked at one wall which was filled from floor to ceiling with bags of sugar.

"You must sell an awful lot of sugar, Richard. You've got tons of it here."

The owner glanced at the inventory. "I don't sell more than a cup a month, Bob. But that sugar salesman," Richard said admiringly, "he can sell sugar!"

••••••••••••

Clint looked over at his business partner Marvin, who had just put down the phone.

"Marvin, you look sick. What's the matter?"

Marvin lifted his head from his hands. "First, my laundry called and said they lost my shirt. Then my broker called to tell me the same thing!"

••••••••••••

Q. What's the difference between cheating on your wife and cheating on your taxes?

A. If you tell the truth on your taxes, the IRS will still want to screw you!

••••••••••••

Taylor had his coat on and was heading for the parking lot when his boss stopped him.

"Spencer, how come you were the last in this morning and now you're the first to leave work?"

"Gee, Mr. Perkins, I didn't want to make the same mistake twice in one day!"

• • • • • • • • • • • •

Bart had left Kansas for college in the East. Six years later, armed with a diploma from Harvard Business School, he landed a high-priced job with a Boston bank. He wired home to his parents:

Have great job and am now making more than Dad ever did. A real feather in my cap.

Three months later he sent another wire: *Given a bonus after just three months. Another feather in my cap.*

After three months had passed, he wired again: *Am the youngest vice-president of the firm. A feather in my cap.*

A few weeks later, another wire: *Have just been fired. Please wire money so I can fly home.*

His parents wired back: *No ticket necessary. Use feathers.*

My rise to the top was through sheer ability and inheritance.

Malcolm Forbes

"It's a vice-president thing, Berger. You wouldn't understand."

•••••••••••

Q. How many corporate research heads does it take to screw in a light bulb?

A. One. But he'll need three outside consultants for that.

•••••••••••

Horace died and moments later arrived at the Pearly Gates where he was greeted by St. Peter.

St. Peter consulted his printout. "Horace, we have an equal opportunity policy in effect now. You get to tour both Heaven and Hell and then you can choose which one you want to spend eternity in. Are you ready to see Heaven?"

Horace nodded and followed St. Peter through the Gates. Heaven was very green and lush with the sun shining down on people in white robes lounging about, reading, playing croquet, or resting. "Seems sort of quiet," Horace opined.

"Yes it is," agreed St. Peter, leading him back to the Pearly Gates where a grinning red Devil awaited.

"C'mon, Horace," said the Devil stepping into an elevator. Seconds later the doors opened to a huge noisy cocktail party. People were dancing, talking, embracing, ordering more drinks. Horace looked around open-mouthed.

"This is great!" he shouted to the Devil who just smiled and nodded.

The next morning Horace was back at the Pearly Gates to make his decision.

"Hell it is," he said emphatically. The Devil grinned and led him to the elevator. When the doors opened, they were greeted by a blast of fire and brimstone.

"Wait a minute, Devil," cried Horace, "what about that scene yesterday?"

"Oh, that was just our summer intern program."

• • • • • • • • • • • •

Brissie called his new secretary into his office and proceeded to dictate a letter to her. At the end of ten minutes he finished and looked.

"Got everything, Miss Tingley?"

"Yes, Mr. Brissie. I'm just missing one thing. Let me go and get a pencil."

• • • • • • • • • • •

The two businessmen met on the street.

The first asked, "How's business?"

"It's okay, can't complain. How's yours?"

"Don't ask," the first replied.

"Oh, really," the other said. Then he thought a second and brightened. "Hey, for this time of year that's not bad!"

• • • • • • • • • • •

The personnel manager called the applicant's previous employer to get an opinion of the applicant's work habits.

"Was he a steady employee?" the manager asked.

"Steady? He was practically motionless!"

• • • • • • • • • • •

Executive: A man who has an infinite capacity for taking planes.

••••••••••••

A young man applied for a job with a fast-growing Silicon Valley computer company. The personnel manager, overworked and swamped with resumes and phone calls, looked over the young man's application.

"This is it, huh? Get some experience and come back in five years."

The young man smiled brightly. "Would morning or afternoon be better?"

••••••••••••

"The job is yours," said the company vice-president. "It pays $18,000 a year to start."

The man looked dubious. "Eighteen thousand, huh. I was looking for something like $25,000 a year."

"We couldn't pay that much," the vice-president protested. You're replacing a very competent and experienced person who was making $19,000."

"Yes, but she had talent and I don't. That's what makes the job so much harder for me!"

•••••••••••

Guidelines for bureaucrats:
(1) When in charge, ponder.
(2) When in trouble, delegate.
(3) When in doubt, mumble.

James H. Boren

•••••••••••

Tarzan arrived home, climbed the vine, slumped down on a tree stump, and poured himself a tall scotch. Jane looked on disapprovingly.

"Tarzan, every day you come home and pour yourself a big drink. I'm concerned."

"I can't help it, Jane. It's a jungle out there."

•••••••••••

An accountant went to his optometrist to see if he needed a prescription for glasses. The optometrist examined the man and then pulled down an eye chart.

"Cover your right eye and read the bottom line."
"Before or after taxes?"

••••••••••••

The executive secretary was transferred from her company's headquarters in New York City to the new branch in Houston. Her new boss greeted her as she came in to the office.

"Welcome, Ms. Chipps. I'm Mr. Mecoy. When I show you around the office I think you'll find things are the same here as in New York."

"Well, then kiss me and let's get started."

••••••••••••

Three women were having their hair done and very soon the conversation turned to their sons in college.

"My son is brilliant," proudly stated the first. "Tops in his class at Harvard. He's going to be a doctor."

"My son is doing okay at State," admitted the second. "He should graduate in five years and then he wants to be a lawyer."

"My son is a bit retarded and is having a some trouble with junior college," said the third. "But it's alright. He's going to be an accountant."

• • • • • • • • • • • •

Q. How many personnel managers does it take to screw in a light bulb?

A. Two. One to assure that everything possible is being done while the other screws the light bulb into the water faucet.

• • • • • • • • • • • •

The new publisher of the small-town weekly was trying without success to convince a local store owner to advertise in the paper.

"I've been in the same location for forty years," declared the store owner, "and I've never needed to advertise."

"Excuse me," insisted the publisher, "do you hear

anything?"

The store owner listened. "Yes, those are the bells ringing at the Baptist church."

"Is that an old church?" queried the publisher.

"Historic! Been there a hundred years."

The publisher smiled. "They still ring the bells!"

• • • • • • • • • • • •

I'd like to be rich enough to throw soap away after the letters are worn off.

Andy Rooney

• • • • • • • • • • • •

The boss met Frank, one of his employees, at the coffee wagon.

"Say, Frank, how long does it take you to get to work in the morning?"

"Oh, about an hour after I arrive at the office!"

••••••••••••

The farmer was showing his banker around the farm and trying to impress him with his success so that his loan would be approved. He showed him the various barns, the acres of wheat, and the cattle grazing in the fields.

"I guess that's your hired hand," said the banker pointing to a man near the cattle.

"No, no. That's our first vice-president in charge of cows!"

••••••••••••

A man walked into a savings and loan and walked up to an officer's desk.

"I'd like to see someone about a loan."

"Great," smiled the officer. "How much can you let us have?"

"Belknap, is that a pierced ear I see?"

• • • • • • • • • • •

The two CEOs were having a heated discussion about the proper way to make love. The first CEO stated that it was 75 percent work and 25 percent pleasure. The second CEO insisted that it was 90 percent work and the rest pleasure. Neither one was making any headway in the argument when one spotted a secretary at a desk near the conference room.

"I'm sure this secretary will help us settle the argument," said one. They then carefully stated their sides of the case and asked the woman which CEO did she think was correct.

"You're both wrong," the secretary said wearily. "If there was any work involved you'd have us doing it for you!"

• • • • • • • • • • •

The Journal reporter was interviewing the corporation president about his success.

"I've always felt that money and compensation were the least important parts of my job," droned the executive, lighting up an $8 cigar. "Working long hours to the best of my ability is more rewarding than my salary and bonus package."

"And you became a success after you convinced yourself of this?" asked the reporter.

"No, after I convinced my employees!"

• • • • • • • • • • •

Q. How many corporate vice-presidents does it take to screw in a light bulb?

A. None. We contract out for that.

• • • • • • • • • • •

The two clerks were eating lunch at the coffee shop.

"An article in the *Journal* says that pretty soon all money transactions will be handled by computers. Checks will be a thing of the past and that we will live in a totally cashless society."

"I'm ahead of the curve," sighed the other. "I'm cashless right now."

•••••••••••

A business consultant called a plumber to come and fix the jammed faucets in the wash basin in the executive's bathroom. The plumber arrived and the consultant showed him to the bathroom. The workman looked over the fixtures, peered under the sink, then reached into his bag and took out a hammer. Then he hit the cold water pipe as hard as he could and immediately water started flowing freely. He then scrawled out a bill and handed it to the consultant.

"This is outrageous. You were just here for a few minutes," cried the consultant. "What did you do for $300.50?"

The plumber took back the bill and itemized it:

1) wear and tear on hammer: $.50

2) knowing where to hit: $300.00

•••••••••••

The taxpayer: That's someone who works for the federal government but doesn't have to take a civil service exam.

Ronald Reagan

••••••••••••

"You must be very proud of the business you've built up, Sam," said his neighbor admiringly.

"Oh yes," said Sam. "When I came to this country and opened the business I had a hundred and twenty dollars in my pocket. Now, thirty years later, I'm a tremendous success. I have a factory and five hundred employees, and I'm a half million dollars in debt!"

••••••••••••

A man was being interviewed for a job by the personnel manager.

"I got paid $35,000 in my previous job. In addition, there was full medical coverage, family dental plan, paid leave for maternity, a year-end bonus, six weeks of vacation, and Fridays off in the summer."

"That's terrific," said the personnel manager, "why did you leave the company?"

"They went broke."

••••••••••••

Q. Why did God make gentiles?

A. Someone had to buy retail.

••••••••••••

A man was being interviewed for a job as a prison guard.

"This is a difficult and sometimes dangerous job," said the warden. "Do you think you can handle these men?"

"Don't worry about a thing," assured the applicant. "If these guys give me any trouble, they're outa here."

••••••••••••

"So you got fired today by your supervisor, huh, Eddie. What happened?" asked the sympathetic bartender.

"You know how the supervisor is the one who stands around and watches other people work?"

stated Eddie.

The bartender nodded.

"He got jealous of me. I was standing around so much people thought I was the supervisor!"

• • • • • • • • • • •

Invest in inflation. It is the only thing going up.

Will Rogers

• • • • • • • • • • •

The town's richest man met with the minister after the Sunday service.

"Why does everyone call me cheap and stingy?" complained the man. "I've told everyone I'm leaving half my money to the church when I die."

The minister nodded. "It reminds me of the story about the pig and the cow.

"The cow was much loved by the farmer and his neighbors, while the pig was not popular at all. The pig could not understand this and asked the cow about it.

"'How come you are so well-liked? People say

you're generous and good because you give milk and butter and cream every day. But I give more than that. From me they get bacon and ham; they even pickle my feet. Yet I'm not popular and you are. Why do you think that is?' The cow looked down at the pig and answered, 'Perhaps it's because I give while I'm still alive.'"

• • • • • • • • • • • •

Q. How many Japanese businessmen does it take to screw in a light bulb?

A. Three. One to make sure the new bulb is Japanese, one to change the bulb, and one to look into the export potential of the old bulb.

• • • • • • • • • • • •

The bank president rushed from his office to see what all the noise was about. He grabbed the vice-president who was standing with his arms in the air.

"What's all the commotion?" demanded the

president.

"There's a bank robbery going on," hissed the vice-president.

"Oh, thank goodness," sighed the president, "I thought it was a hostile takeover."

• • • • • • • • • • •

At the Ace Manufacturing Company, with one exception, everyone from president on down to the lowliest worker had signed the new pension plan. But the plan needed total participation or it would not be implemented. For several weeks fellow workers, the personnel manager, and the line supervisor had pleaded, argued and discussed the benefits of the new plan with Ben, the stubborn holdout. All without success. Finally, the president of Ace asked Ben to come to his office.

"Sit down, Ben. I know everyone has talked to you about the new pension plan and you've said no. But here it is and I want you to sign it. If you don't, you're fired."

Without hesitation, Ben picked up a pen and signed the new plan.

"I'm curious, Ben," said the president. "Why didn't you sign it before?"

"Nobody ever explained it as well as you did."

•••••••••••

The worst job I ever had was working in a Fotomat booth. I was the only one at the Christmas party.

Mark Dobrient

•••••••••••

The town's richest man was being interviewed by a reporter for the local paper.

"I owe all my success to a strong will," said the rich man.

"Your strong will?" asked the reporter.

"Not mine, my father's. He died and left me everything in his will."

•••••••••••

Three businessmen—a Frenchman, an American and a Japanese—were captured by terrorists and sentenced to be shot. They were blindfolded and then the head of the terrorists asked each if they had one last request.

"I'd like to sing 'God Save the Queen'," answered the Englishman.

The Japanese then stepped forward. "I'd like to give a speech about the hard-working Japanese people, their commitment to education, and their dedication to quality in the products they produce."

The American stepped forward. "I'd like to be executed ahead of the Japanese so that I don't have to hear another speech about Japanese quality!"

• • • • • • • • • • •

To sell something, tell a woman it's a bargain; tell a man it's deductible.

Earl Wilson

• • • • • • • • • • •

"Miss Frobish, you're late again," admonished her supervisor. "Is there any reason for this constant tardiness?"

"Yes, Mr. Rhodes. It makes the day shorter."

• • • • • • • • • • •

A department store salesman was on his lunch break and ran into an old friend who used to work at the same store.

"Jarvis, how are things going?" asked the second man.

"Okay Barry," said the salesman. "I see you're wearing a police uniform."

"Yeah, I went through the academy and now I'm a cop."

"How do you like that?"

"Well, the hours are pretty good, and the pay's okay, but what I really like about it is that the customer is always wrong!"

• • • • • • • • • • •

The stock market was fluctuating so wildly that Dave, a stock broker, could not leave the office until eleven o'clock. He decided to check into the Wall Street Hotel rather than take the commuter train all the way out to Huntington.

"I'd like a room," Dave said to the hotel clerk.

"Fine sir. For jumping or for sleeping?"

•••••••••••

Q. Why is the stock market like an oven?

A. They can both be self-cleaning.

•••••••••••

October is one of the peculiarly dangerous months to speculate in stocks. The others are July, January, September, April, November, May, March, June, December, August, and February.

Mark Twain

•••••••••••

Frank Persons, whose business was selling millions of chickens a day, had a brilliant marketing idea to help sell more poultry. He called the Vatican and requested a private audience with the Pope. The request was granted and a few weeks later Mr. Persons was ushered into a room for his meeting with the Pontiff.

After explaining who he was, Mr. Persons began. "Your Eminence, I have a proposition to make that I think will help both of us. I'd like you to change the words of The Lord's Prayer from 'give us this day our daily bread' to 'give us this day our daily chicken.' It'll sell a lot more chickens and I'm prepared to pay the Church a million dollars for this."

The Pope shook his head vehemently and said, "No, I'm afraid that's quite impossible."

Frank persisted, "Well, would you take ten million dollars to make the change?"

Again the Pope shook his head. "Mr. Persons, The Lord's Prayer has remained essentially unchanged for a thousand years. We can't tamper with it."

Persons raised his offer. "Will you take one hundred million dollars?"

This was a huge amount of money and the Pope, aware of the needs of the poor, the hungry, the missions, and the myriad other financial burdens of the Church, thought for a moment before answering.

"Mr. Persons, you've got a deal."

A meeting of the College of Cardinals was quickly convened by the Pope.

"My dear colleagues," the Pope began. "I have some good news and some bad news. The good news is that we are receiving one hundred million dollars from Mr. Frank Persons to change The

Lord's Prayer from 'give us this day our daily bread' to 'give us this day our daily chicken.' The bad news is that we're losing the Wonder Bread account."

• • • • • • • • • • •

Ed ran into his friend Mel at a local bar.

"Mel, how's the new job going at the computer factory?"

Mel took a drink of beer. "I'm through with it, Ed."

"What happened?"

"Oh, the swearing on the job, the tardiness, the sloppiness in the workmanship, not caring... " Mel shook his head disgustedly. "They just couldn't put up with it anymore!"

• • • • • • • • • • •

"Bill, you're late again for work," said the foreman as Bill punched in. "What is the reason for the tardiness?"

"Well, you see, boss, the alarm woke up everyone

in the house except me," said Bill.

"I don't understand. How could the alarm wake up everyone except you?"

"There are eight in our house," explained Bill. "And the alarm was set for seven!"

••••••••••••

"I was talking to the president of the company in the elevator today," the man said to his wife.

"Oh, did he say anything?"

"He told me that he was surrounded by 'yes' men."

"What did you say?"

"I agreed with him!"

••••••••••••

Retirement at sixty-five is ridiculous. When I was sixty-five I still had pimples.

George Burns

••••••••••••

Heifitz came to this country from Riga when he was thirteen years old and soon got a job as a ribbon salesman. After fifty-five years as the company's best salesman he was retiring in three weeks. He had accomplished everything he had set out to do, with one exception. For forty years he tried to crack the Abercrombie Dry Goods store, one of the biggest retailers in his territory. One last time he approached the store's buying office.

"Mr. Abercrombie, in a couple of weeks I'll be retiring to Florida. For forty years I've been calling on you and you've always refused to give me an order. It would make complete my career if I could just get one last small order before I leave."

Abercrombie leaned across the desk. "Alright, Heifitz. One order. I'd like some bright red, two-inch wide, heavy-vellum brocaded ribbon. Think you can do that?"

"No problem, Mr. Abercrombie," smiled Heifitz. "What length?"

"From the tip of your nose to the tip of your penis," Abercrombie snarled.

Heifitz gulped. "It'll be here in two weeks."

Two weeks later, Heifitz walked into the Abercrombie warehouse. Everywhere, from floor to ceiling, aisle upon aisle, he saw bright red, two-inch wide, heavy-vellum brocaded ribbon. A moment later, a heavy hand on his shoulder spun him around.

"Heifitz, what's the big idea!" yelled a red-faced Abercrombie. "You lied to me. Look at all this ribbon."

"Is it the wrong color, Mr. Abercrombie?"

"It's not the color, Heifitz. I wanted it to stretch from the tip of your nose to the tip of your penis."

"That's right, Mr. Abercrombie. The tip of my nose is here and the tip of my penis is in Poland."

• • • • • • • • • • • •

How can I believe in God when just last week I got my tongue caught in the roller of an electric typewriter?

Woody Allen